Nicholas Comes to America the Story of Santa Claus

By: Terry & Laura Lynch

Illustrated by: Ellen R. Lynch

Nicholas Comes to America the Story of Santa Claus

Copyright © 2010

All rights reserved. No part of this book shall be reproduced, stored or transmitted by any means without the sole written permission of the author.

ISBN: 978-0-578-07294-4

Printed in the U.S.A. by: HFK Presents Publishing

Dedicated to our parents:

Edgar & Loretta Hield
and Dennis & Mary Lynch

For wonderful family Christmases

Table of Contents

Forward

Introduction

Chapter 1
Boy Bishop of Myra

Chapter 2
The Legend Grows

Chapter 3
Nicholas and His Legend Travel the World

Chapter 4
Symbols & Traditions of Christmas

Chapter 5
The Twelve Days of Christmas

Epilogue
Family Recipes
Christmas Journal
Recommended Reading

Forward

One of the central characters in any child's Christmas celebration is St. Nicholas or Santa Claus. As editor Francis Pharcellus Church of the New York Sun stated in a letter to eight year old Virginia O'Hanlon in 1897, "Yes, Virginia, there is a Santa Claus. He exists as certainly as love and generosity and devotion exist, and you know that they abound and give to your life its highest beauty and joy. Alas! How dreary would be the world if there were no Santa Claus. It would be as dreary as if there were no Virginias." Little Virginia was concerned because some of her friends had begun to scoff at the idea of the jolly old elf. He continued by saying "No Santa Claus! Thank God he lives, and he lives forever. A thousand years from now, Virginia, nay, ten times ten thousand years from now, he will continue to make glad the heart of childhood." Few of us could argue with Mr. Church.

St. Nicholas of Myra was most certainly a real person, born in the area of present day Turkey in approximately 270AD. The stories, traditions, and symbols of this saint are a combination of stories, both written and oral, as well as cultural traditions.

This book is meant to bring a deeper meaning and understanding of the Christmas season to young and old alike. Questions as to *why* certain traditions are celebrated are as varied as the families who celebrate them!

Why not take this little book and read a portion of it a day in the weeks leading up to Christmas? Children –while we can't deny them the secular excitement of the holiday – might also come to understand the spiritual anticipation of the feast. In this way, they will have a better understanding of not only the origins of the jolly ol' elf, but of the reasons why we decorate Christmas trees, or hang stockings, etc.

Family traditions are very important, and this book provides an opportunity to share not only beloved family Christmas recipes, but cherished memories of Christmases gone by. Merry Christmas to all!

Christmas presents were known in antiquity among kings and chieftains, especially on the European continent. However, they have been common among ordinary people in Iceland only during the past 100 or so years.

Introduction

The Christmas holidays are a wonderful time of year. They are a time for getting together with family and friends to remember the meaning of the season; the birth of the Jesus.

The season brings with it traditions and customs, some of which date back to pagan times. Each of the traditions of Christmas hold time honored places of reverence in our hearts. Whether you hang stockings by the fireplace, exchange gifts, or feast on a Christmas goose, Christmas just wouldn't seem like Christmas if they were excluded from our celebrations. Where did these traditions begin? Why do we still hold them so dear?

At the heart of the celebration is the Christ Child. This innocent babe brings with him the hopes and dreams of salvation and love each year during the holiday season. It is during this holy time that we feel that "special something" in the air. It is a time when we take a moment to stop and look at our neighbor with a measure of compassion unlike that at any other time of year.

The incarnation of that feeling, that hope in humanity is represented by none other than St. Nicholas.

Nicholas is a ***real person***. Through the centuries, he has taken many forms throughout the world dressed in the clothing of the country and culture to make its people feel truly special. He is the messenger of Christ's love. Nicholas gives us a yearly reminder of how we should follow the two most important commandments: *"Thou shalt love the Lord thy God with all thy heart, and with all thy soul, and with thy entire mind. This is the first and greatest commandment. And the second is like unto it. Thou shalt love thy neighbor as thyself. On these two commandments hang all the law and the prophets."* *[Matt22:37-40]*

So whether it is St. Nicholas, Father Christmas, Grandfather Frost, or Santa Claus you look for during the holiday season, remember why this messenger comes to us; he brings the message of love from the Christ Child.

Saint Francis of Assisi is credited with creating the first nativity scene, as a way to make the Christmas season a time of peace and goodwill.

1. Boy Bishop of Myra

The story of Nicholas, Bishop of Myra begins with his birth a long time ago in a small town called Patara (PAT-ar-ah). Nicholas was an only child adored by his mother and father. For many years, his parents were unable to have a child. Throughout that time, Nicholas' mother had prayed to Jesus for a child to love. Eventually, his parents were blessed with the gift of Nicholas. His mother wanted to thank Jesus for giving her a son. As he was growing up, Nicholas' mother always told him that he was a special gift from God, and he should always honor Jesus as a way to thank him.

Unfortunately, While Nicholas was still young, his parents died, leaving him an orphan. However, they left him a good deal of money as an inheritance.

Remembering his mother's teachings to always honor Jesus, Nicholas thought the best thing he could do would be to become a priest. He traveled to Myra to start his journey to priesthood as an altar boy. When he arrived in Myra, it was too late in the day to get into the cathedral. He spent the night sleeping on the steps of the church.

What he did not know, was that the elders of the church had had a dream that night. In that dream, they were told the first person to come through the doors of the cathedral the next morning would become the bishop. When Nicholas awoke, he opened the doors to the cathedral, and was made Bishop of all Myra. He was known as Nicholas the Boy Bishop, because he was so young.

After receiving this honor, Nicholas promised to honor Jesus in every way. He felt the best way to do this would be to lead by example; doing good deeds for others, expecting nothing in return.

One of the most famous examples of Nicholas' good deeds was the time he secretly helped a man and his three daughters. There was a man in town, who had fallen on hard times, and had lost his wife. He was raising his three daughters on his own.

When the oldest daughter wanted to get married, the man had no money to give as a dowry. Long ago, a dowry was money, property or material goods a bride's family gave to a bridegroom or his family at the time of wedding. If a bride did not have a dowry, she could not get married.

The man thought if he sold his daughter into slavery, he could use the money as dowries for his two other daughters when they wanted to get married.

Nicholas found out about the poor man's situation, and the night before the oldest daughter was about to be sold, he took some of his own money that was left to him by his parents, wrapped it into a ball in his handkerchief, snuck out to the man's house in the dark of night when no one would see him, and threw the money into the window of the house.

The next morning, the man woke up, found the money, and used it for his daughter's dowry and wedding. She was not sold into slavery. The man was so happy for the gift, that he asked everyone in the town who had done this wondrous deed, so he could thank them. No one in the town knew who had thrown the money into the man's window.

Time went by, and the man's second daughter wanted to get married. He was still down on his luck and had no money. He thought if he sold his second daughter into slavery, he would have money for his third daughter's dowry.

Again, Nicholas heard of the poor man's situation. The night before she was about to be sold into slavery, he took some of his money, put it into his handkerchief, tied it into

a ball, snuck out to the man's house in the dead of night, and threw the money into the window, making sure he was not seen by anyone.

The next morning, the man woke up, found the money, and was able to save his second daughter from slavery, as well as pay for her wedding and dowry. Once again he asked around town, but no one would take credit for helping the man with his financial difficulties.

Unfortunately, the man continued to suffer hard times, and when it came time for the third daughter to marry, he had no money. Once again, he thought if he sold this daughter into slavery, at least *she* would be cared for.

The night before she was about to be sold, Nicholas once again came with his handkerchief full of money. Carefully, he crept up to the house. Just before he threw the money into the window, the man jumped out of the shadows, grabbed his arm, and said "Bishop Nicholas, is it you who has saved my children from slavery?" Bishop Nicholas admitted that it was he who had thrown the money in the window. The man was so grateful; he wanted the world to know of Nicholas' wondrous deeds.

However, Nicholas said that if he really wanted to make him happy, keep this as their little secret and instead, do good deeds for others, *expecting nothing in return.*

Nicholas said that this would make both him and Jesus very happy. He told the man that if he did this, he would be rewarded tenfold. However, Nicholas told the man that when the time was right, he would allow him to tell people what he had done for him. This is how Nicholas came to be known as the giver of gifts, and the protector of children.

Nicholas left gifts in the middle of the night, unseen by children, and expected nothing in return. That is how his legend began.

The abbreviation of Xmas for Christmas is not irreligious. The first letter of the word Christ in Greek is chi, which is identical to our X. Xmas was originally an ecclesiastical abbreviation that was used in tables and charts.

2. The Legend Grows

As time went on, stories of the boy bishop of Myra continued to grow and spread throughout the land. One such story is of Nicholas and the three generals. This legend is set during the reign of the Emperor Constantine when Nicholas was bishop of Myra. Constantine sent three generals to settle some unrest in a distant area of the Roman Empire. While on their way, the generals and their soldiers ran into a storm and had to stop over in Andriaki, which was the port of Myra. While they were waiting for the weather to clear, the troops went into port and eventually into Myra.

While in Myra, the soldiers began to fight and argue. Before matters got worse, Nicholas went to the generals and asked them to restore order. The generals were unaware until that moment that the trouble was being caused by their own troops! They rushed into town and put an end to the fighting. Nicholas blessed them, and walked them back to the port of Myra.

Nicholas was about to depart, when he saw a group of men and women weeping.

When he asked what was wrong, he was told of a dishonest official who was preparing to execute three innocent men.

Nicholas and the generals rushed to the place where the men were to be executed. Just before the execution was to take place, Nicholas grabbed the sword out of the executioner's hands. At this, the dishonest official admitted to his wrong doing and begged for Nicholas's forgiveness. Nicholas forgave the official, and they parted peacefully.

The generals headed on their way to settle the unrest Emperor Constantine had sent them to take care of in the first place. They peacefully settled the area, and reported back to Constantine that the disturbance had been settled without blood shed. Constantine rewarded them with gifts and a higher rank. This caused the generals' enemies in Constantine's court to become jealous.

The Imperial Chancellor of the court went to Constantine, and lied about the generals forming an army to overthrow him. Constantine believed the Chancellor, and the generals were imprisoned and set to be executed.

They remembered how Nicholas had saved the three men who had been wrongly blamed, and prayed for his help. On the night before they were about to die, Nicholas appeared to Constantine in a dream and showed him how the generals had been falsely accused.

Nicholas also appeared to the Chancellor, and told him he must confess his lie. Constantine heeded the dream and released the generals. He told them that they should visit the bishop and gave them a gold covered Bible to give to Nicholas. They went to Nicholas to thank him for saving their lives. Nicholas said they should not thank *him*, they should thank the Lord. In thanksgiving to the Lord for their miraculous rescue, the three generals became monks.

Nicholas' association with the number three dates back to time of the Nicene Council in 325AD. Emperor Constantine convened the first Ecumenical Council, where more than 300 bishops came from all over the Christian world to debate the Holy Trinity and establish the foundation of the Christian church. It was a very controversial and contentious meeting.

At one point, Arius (AR-ee-uhs) of Alexandria taught that Jesus was not equal to God the Father.

He therefore argued that the Trinity should not be taught. The bishops listened respectfully, but Nicholas became troubled. Rage finally overtook him and he stood up, crossed the chambers and slapped Arius across the face. The bishops were shocked and brought Nicholas before Constantine. The Emperor had a law that said it was illegal for anyone to strike a bishop.

Constantine felt the *bishops* should determine Nicholas's punishment because he himself was a bishop. The bishops' decision was to strip Nicholas of his bishop's garments, chain him up and throw him in jail. Nicholas would not be allowed to attend the meetings, and when the council was finished, they would decide Nicholas' fate. Nicholas was ashamed and prayed for forgiveness. Through it all, he continued to believe the Holy Trinity was three in one; Father, Son and Holy Spirit.

During the night, Jesus and Mary appeared to Nicholas asking, "Why are you in jail?" His response was "Because of my love for you." Jesus gave a book of the Gospels to Nicholas, and Mary gave him his bishop's garments. Nicholas was once again dressed as a bishop, and at peace.

Throughout the night, he studied the Scriptures. The next morning, the jailer came to Nicholas' cell and found the chains on the floor and Nicholas dressed in his bishop's robes, reading the Scriptures. When word made it to Constantine, he freed Nicholas and allowed him to return to the council-- reinstated as Bishop of Myra.

The council saw this as a sign that Nicholas was teaching the true interpretation of the Trinity and sided with Nicholas, not Arius. The council produced the Nicene Creed, which Christians repeat weekly as their beliefs.

Another tale recalls a time when throughout the land, the crops failed and Myra fell victim to famine. As the bishop and shepherd of his flock, Nicholas became very concerned for the welfare of his people. He worked desperately to find grain to feed his community.

At one point, ships bound for Alexandria with a cargo of wheat, anchored in the port of Myra. Nicholas asked the captain for some grain for his people. The captain said he could not give him any grain because it had already been weighed and measured. He told Nicholas that when he arrived in Alexandria, his grain would have to weigh the same as when it was first measured. Nicholas assured him not to worry, the weight and measure would be the same, if only he would give him some grain.

The captain was worried he would be in trouble for the shortage, but was finally assured by Nicholas to trust him and all would be well. The captain gave Nicholas 400 bushels of grain. He then set sail for Alexandria. When the captain arrived in Alexandria, the grain was unloaded and measured, and there was *no* shortage.

The captain explained what he had done in Myra, and all were convinced that Nicholas had performed a miracle. As for the 400 bushels Nicholas received, he used it to feed the people of Myra for two years until the famine subsided. He even had enough grain to provide seed for a good harvest.

Another wonderful story of St. Nicholas was when he took a pilgrimage, or trip, to Jerusalem to walk in the footsteps of Jesus. Knowing other Christians might feel a bit ill at ease traveling with a bishop, he chose to sail in a boat from Egypt. The Egyptians would consider him a man like any other; the title of bishop meaning nothing to non-Christians.

While they were at sea, a tremendous storm arose. Clouds darkened the sky, the winds picked up, and huge waves came over the sides of the ship. The crew was convinced they would die at sea.

Nicholas calmed the sailors by telling them to "Pray with me to my Lord, and we will be saved." As they prayed, the storm calmed. The winds died down and the waves returned to the sea. All on board rejoiced proclaiming Nicholas' God as their savior.

However, when they returned to the deck above, they found that one sailor, who was trying to tighten the sails on the mast, had fallen during the storm and lay dead upon the deck. Nicholas knew he must perform a miracle to convert the now doubting sailors to Christianity. He approached the man as though he were sleeping and said, "Wake up, no need to sleep, the storm is over."

At that moment, the man awoke as if he had not been dead, but asleep. Once again, the sailors rejoiced! Convinced they had witnessed a miracle, the crew converted to Christianity. As a result of this miracle, Nicholas became known as the Patron Saint of Sailors.

Whenever a ship wanted safe passage, sailors would pray to Saint Nicholas. Likewise, when a ship arrived safely in port, the mariners would thank the Saint of Sailors.

The story of Nicholas began to spread, and when seamen in a port were unfamiliar with Nicholas and asked about this great man; sailors would retell the stories and legends of Nicholas' life. This is how the legend traveled to the four corners of the world.

Nicholas wanted people around the world to feel comfortable and at ease around him. He would allow them to call him by whatever name they chose. He appeared to people around the world dressed in a way that would be considered appropriate for their country or culture. This is the reason why he is known by many different names throughout the world including, among others: Santa Claus, Father Christmas, Pere Noel, or Grandfather Frost. He also appears in clothing appropriate for the climate or culture of a country.

*In North American poetry and illustrations, Santa Claus, in his white beard, red jacket and pompom-topped cap, would sally forth on the night before Christmas in his sleigh, pulled by eight reindeer, and climb down chimneys to leave his gifts in stockings children set out on the fireplace's mantelpiece.*

3. Nicholas and His Legend Travel the World

Sailors traveling the world brought the legends of St. Nicholas with them to their various ports of call. The people of these towns and villages would see the sailors praying to Nicholas for safe passage of their vessels. The town's people would ask the sailors about Nicholas. That is how Nicholas' legend grew.

After he became bishop, Nicholas promised God that he would set an example for his flock to lead a good Christian life. The stories of Nicholas brought him to countries all around the world. This was the perfect opportunity for Nicholas to bring his promise to all!

He never wanted people to feel ill at ease because he was a bishop. He wanted to bring Jesus' message of love and giving to all. He wanted to inspire others to perform good deeds, without expecting anything in return. How would he do this? The world is a pretty big place! The people of the world don't look the same-- they dress differently, speak different languages, and have different traditions. What a wonderful stew of cultures!

This is the reason why Nicholas is known by many names, and appears with different helpers in many styles of clothing. Beginning with his feast day on December 6th, and continuing through the Feast of the Epiphany on January 6th, St. Nicholas has become a beloved part of many celebrations throughout the world. Let's take a look at some of the fun!

In the county of **Greece**, St. Nicholas is called **Nikolaos** or *Agios Vailios*. His clothes are soaked with brine and his beard is dripping wet. As the protector of sailors and seamen, his face is covered with perspiration as he tries to reach sinking ships and save men from drowning.

Christmas trees are not traditional symbols in Greek homes. Rather, the symbol of Christmas in Grecian homes is a clay bowl with a piece of wire suspended across the top. Hanging from the wire is a sprig of basil tied around a wooden cross, and below the cross, to keep the basil fresh is a bit of holy water.

Greek tradition says that during the twelve day period, from Christmas to the Feast of the Epiphany on January 6th, the Killantzaroi, a type of goblin, rises from the center of the earth to cause mischief.

In order to keep the mischief causing goblins away, once a day someone in the family dips the cross into the holy water in the bowl, and uses it to bless each room of the house. The fireplace is kept lit continuously during this time as well. Fasting is required during the 40 days before Christmas, so when the big day finally arrives it brings with it great celebrating!

On Christmas Eve, children go from door to door singing carols and giving people good blessings for the coming year. They are rewarded for their performances, which often include drums and pipe instruments, with candy and fruits. On January 6th--St. Basil's Day, also the Epiphany is the day gifts are exchanged.

The country of *Italy* calls St. Nicholas **Babbo Natale**, or Old Man Christmas. He is dressed in his traditional bishop's miter and cloak, and travels with a donkey.

Italy holds a special place for St. Nicholas, particularly the *Basilica San Nicolas* in Bari, Italy. After the *Church of St. Nicholas* in Myra, the Basilica has become a church where many people make a special pilgrimage to honor this very special saint.

During the Christmas season, small presents are drawn from a container known as the "Urn of Fate". The "Urn of Fate" is part of the Christmas celebrations in many Italian households. It is brought out on Christmas Eve, and holds a wrapped present for everyone.

The mother tries her luck first, followed by others in the family. If you get a present with your name on it, you keep it; otherwise, you put it back and try again.

The main gift exchange takes place on January 6th, the feast of the Epiphany, which commemorates the visit of the Magi to the baby Jesus.

In Italy, the children wait until Epiphany for their presents and hang up their stockings on January 5th. They nervously await a visit from *La Befana*.

According to the La Befana legend, when the Three Wise Men were on their way to Bethlehem to visit the baby Jesus, they stopped during their journey and asked an old woman for directions. They told her of Jesus' birth and asked her to join them. She said no, and the Wise Men continued on their way. Later, a shepherd asked her to join him in paying respect to the Baby Jesus, and Befana refused again.

Within a few hours, the woman changed her mind and wished she had gone to visit the Christ Child. She arrived at the stable where Jesus was, but could not find him as Joseph and Mary had long departed to escape execution by King Herod, who wanted to kill Jesus.

In Italian folklore, she is called Befana and depicted variously as a fairy queen, a crone, or an ugly witch on a broomstick. Befana is said to have been flying around ever since, looking for the Christ Child each year and leaving presents at every house with children in case he is there. She slides down chimneys, and fills stockings and shoes with gifts for good children and pieces of charcoal for the bad ones.

Spain and Portugal know Nicholas as **San Nicola**, or Pai Natal. In Spain, the Three Wise Men help Nicholas during the Christmas season. On January 6th, they bring the gifts to children who leave their shoes outside filled with straw and barley for their tired camels. In the morning, the straw and barley are replaced with presents.

December 8th begins the season with Los Seises (dance of six), which is an elaborate ritual dance performed by six costumed boys.

The precise gestures and movements of this dance are moving and beautiful.

On Christmas Day, people play on swing sets especially set up for the holidays since swinging at solstice evokes an ancient desire for the sun to "swing" higher in the sky.

On Christmas Eve, Portuguese families gather around the Christmas tree and the crèche to celebrate the birth of Jesus. The crèche is a very important part of the celebration. Traditionally, children are in charge of collecting materials for the crèche. While some families only display the three main figures, Infant Jesus, Virgin Mary and St. Joseph, others design larger scenes with the three figures, the Three Wise Kings, the shepherds, sheep, and lakes (made with mirrors) and hills (made with stones, moss, and clay).

Instead of hanging a stocking on the fireplace, some families put one sapatinho, or shoe, of each child next to the chimney. Most kitchens in Portugal have a chimney; or a fireplace. Many families open the presents displayed around the Christmas tree on Christmas Eve around midnight. Others open them in the morning of the December 25th, Christmas Day.

Children in *France* know St. Nicholas as *Père Noel* or Father Christmas. He is dressed in a long red robe. He travels with a donkey that carries baskets full of treats and toys. Children stuff their shoes with hay and carrots for the reindeers. They hope Père Noel will take the reindeer food, and leave them presents and candy.

In many countries, St. Nicholas has a companion who warns children who have been naughty to change their ways.

In France, St. Nicholas' companion is *Père Fouettard*. He comes from a legend of St. Nicholas that involves three children who wandered away and got lost. Cold and hungry, the children were lured into the shop of a wicked butcher who attacked them and salted away the three in a large tub. Through the help of St. Nicholas, the children were returned to their families. This story led to Nicholas being recognized as the protector of children.

In France, statues and paintings often portray this event, showing the saint with children in a barrel. The evil butcher came to be known as Père Fouettard and he has followed St. Nicholas in shame ever since. It is said that Père Frouettard grows *uglier* with every child's smile he sees!

Many years ago Père Fouettard carried switches or twigs to threaten children. These days, he is feared more because he is the person who tells St. Nicholas about children who have been naughty!

On the eve of St. Nicholas Day, children put their shoes near the chimney and sing a song to Saint Nicholas before going off to bed. The shoes overflow in the morning with special Saint Nicholas sweet treats—chocolates and special cookies. No child is perfect, so even good children find ribbon-tied birch twigs.

In **Poland**, St. Nicholas is ***Sw. Mikolaj,*** and is dressed as a dignified saintly bishop carrying a crozier or staff. He comes down from heaven with an angel as a companion, and rides a white schimmel, or horse. Nicholas is a jolly character with a twinkle in his eye and a welcoming, booming voice. He talks to the children, praising those who have been good, and correcting those who have been naughty. He gives the children holy pictures, red apples or oranges and special Polish cookies called pierniki.

If the Polish children don't see St. Nicholas in person, he puts treats under their pillows when they are sleeping, or in their freshly cleaned and polished shoes left out the night before. St. Nicholas acts in his traditional religious role as a protector of children and encourages Polish children to be good, as there are switches for naughty children.

In the *Ukraine*, St. Nicholas, or *Sviatyij Mykolai,* comes dressed as a bishop with angels as his companions. He often quizzes children on their catechism before giving them gifts. His icons or pictures are found in nearly every home. In the mountains of Western Ukraine the four seasons of the year are named after saints. Winter honors St. Nicholas.

In *Romania*, St. Nicholas Day is one of the most important holidays. On December 5th, children polish their shoes and leave them out to be filled by St. Nicholas, or *Sfantul Nicolae.* On the sixth of December, gifts are given to friends, children, and those in need.

In the *Czech Republic*, angels lower St. Nicholas, or *Svaty Mikuláš,* with a basket of apples, nuts, and candies, down from heaven on a heavy golden cord. On December 5th, the eve of St. Nicholas Day, three figures—kindly St. Nicholas who gives gifts to children, a devil who comes to take bad children away, and an angel who pleads on their behalf—form a procession marking the beginning of the

Christmas season. The streets are filled with devils rattling chains, St. Nicholases with white cotton beards, long robes and bishops' staffs, and angels with paper wings on their way to visit small children in their homes.

Long ago, St. Nicholas quizzed children on the prayer book and the Bible. Today, the questions are mostly about the previous year's behavior. The angel writes a record for each child in a large book and the children sing or say a poem to the saint. The devil rattles his chains, threatening to carry bad children off, but the angel, with a gold star on her forehead and dressed in a white gown, protects the children. Good children receive stockings filled with tangerines, nuts, chocolates, and small gifts. It is said that bad children get old potatoes or coal in their stockings.

Parents and other relatives also give a St. Nicholas gift, which may be hidden so children must hunt to find it. After the children's treats, St. Nicholas shares a toast with the parents.

In *Russia*, many of the religious celebrations of Christmas are being replaced by the Festival of Winter. Before the 1917 Revolution, celebrations centered mainly on Christmas, while after the revolution, the focus was mainly on the New Year. However, you can still find many of the pre- revolution traditional celebrations.

St. Nicholas is **Ded Moroz**, or Grandfather Frost. He is dressed in a long fur coat covered in beautiful, bright blue cloth trimmed in fur.

As in Italy, he has two companions that travel with him. One is a grandmotherly figure called **Babushka**. Babushka is a traditional Christmas figure who distributes presents to children. Her name means grandmother, and the legend is told that she decided not to go with the wise men to see Jesus because of the cold weather. However, she regretted not going and set off to try and catch up, filling her basket with presents. She never found Jesus, and that is why she visits each house, leaving toys for good children.

St. Nicholas has another companion in Russia by the name of **Snegurochka**, or the Snow Maiden. She is the granddaughter of Grandfather Frost.

St. Nicholas is very popular in Russia. There is a story that the 11th-century Prince Vladimir traveled to Constantinople to be baptized, and returned with stories of miracles performed by St. Nicholas of Myra.

Since then, many Eastern Orthodox Churches have been named for the saint, and to this day, Nicholas is one of the most common names for Russian boys.

A ceremony involving the blessing of the home is frequently observed. A priest visits the home accompanied by boys carrying vessels of holy water. A little water is sprinkled in each room. The kutya, or sweet pudding is eaten from a common dish to symbolize unity.

In some countries, there are *many* traditions. Sometimes, there are traditions for every region of a country. One country that has many traditions is Germany.

In **Austria** and **Germany**, children leave letters on their windowsills for **Christkind**, a winged figure dressed in white robes and a golden crown who gives gifts to children. Sometimes the letters are decorated with glue and sprinkled with sugar to make them sparkle.

December 6th brings St. Nicholas or **Nikolaus.** He arrives on a schimmel or white horse on St. Claus day. A shoe or boot is left outside the door on December 5th with hopes that the following morning presents are found if you have been good, or if you have been naughty… a rod.

In parts of **Germany**, people believe that the Christ Child sends a messenger on Christmas Eve. This messenger appears as an angel in a white robe and crown, bearing gifts. The angel is called ***Christkind***. There is also a Christmas Eve figure called ***Weihnachtsmann*** or Christmas Man. He looks like Santa Claus and also brings gifts. It is the ***Christkind*** who brings the presents, accompanied by one of its many devilish companions, ***Knecht Rupprecht***, ***Pelznickle***, ***Ru-Klas***. These are the companions who warn naughty children to be kind.

The country of ***Switzerland*** welcomes ***Samichlaus*** on December 6th riding a donkey and bringing baskets full of small gifts, fruits and nuts to all of the good children. He is accompanied by ***Schmutzli***, dressed all in black, covered in soot, carrying a switch and a bag to warn the bad children to mend their ways.

When St. Nicholas arrives in ***Great Britain***, he is known as **Father Christmas.** He is dressed in a long red or green coat with a long white beard. He usually wears a wreath of fresh evergreen in his hair. The wreath goes back to the pagan tradition of worshipping the spirits of the forest. Many times, Nicholas took traditions and rituals of pagan religions, and made them Christian. This made the conversion of pagans to Christianity easier; because they were already familiar and comfortable with symbols from their own traditions.

In 17th century England as in other European countries, Christmas celebrations had gotten to be raucous ceremonies at the Lord of the Manor's estate. These celebrations sometimes lasted as long as two weeks! All were invited from beggar to prince. Some dressed in costumes while others danced and caroled. Carolers were rewarded with a "spirited" drink for adults only, which included hot spiced ale, sherry and cognac. They were poured a glass and greeted with the phrase "was hal" which meant "be well". This phrase became "wassail". Carolers began to go "a-wassailing"—singing house to house in hopes of receiving a cup of wassail.

Another practice included bands of costumed and masked men wandering from house to house putting on mummer's plays. Father Christmas would travel on the back of a goat or donkey giving well behaved children gifts or small presents. These festivals added to the excitement of the holiday season.

The Puritans of the time argued that Christ would not have allowed raucous observances which were merely an excuse to sin. Despite these challenges to their merriment, the English adapted their celebrations and made them a more religious observance.

In the 19th century, British author Charles Dickens wrote Christmas stories such as ***A Christmas Carol***, ***The Chimes*** and ***A Cricket on the Hearth***. These popular stories helped to bring Christmas celebrations and the true meaning of Christmas back to its roots. A stamp of approval for these changes came from Queen Victoria, who would annually have a fir tree brought from the Black Forest, decorate it in the royal palace in honor of her husband, Prince Albert of Germany, who had grown up with the German tradition of a decorated Christmas tree.

As a result, Christmas celebrations in England once again included more secular forms of celebrating with caroling, gift giving, and Christmas feasts. The best of both worlds!

In **Sweden**, **Juletomten** brings gifts on a sleigh pulled by Julbocks or the Christmas Goats. He is accompanied by tomtes which are elves or knomes.

The tomtes make ornaments of wheat to decorate trees. Swedish children leave the tomtes porridge in hopes of receiving a gift.

Another tradition in Sweden involves the oldest daughter in the family. On December 13th, St. Lucia Day, the young girl assumes the saint's identity and wears a white gown, with a wreath of green leaves and candles on her head.

St. Lucia was a Sicilian martyr who refused to marry a pagan and gave all her money to the poor. She was thrown in jail, sentenced to death, and while imprisoned awaiting her execution, she brought food to the other prisoners. To light her way through the prison, she wore a crown of candles on her head, so her hands would be free to carry the food to the prisoners.

Her legend spread to Sweden where they now honor her by recreating the giving of food to prisoners. Very early in the morning, the oldest daughter brings coffee and saffron flavored buns to her parent's bedroom and is joined by her brothers and sisters who act as the angels and star boys. The day ends with a candle lit parade and traditional bonfire in town.

This practice dates back to the pagan ritual of driving away evil spirits of darkness with a blazing fire.

The traditions of **Finland** are similar and involve Nicholas, called ***Joulupukki,*** accompanied by elves bringing julklappar or Christmas presents on December 24th to all of the good children.

The Dutch of the ***Netherlands*** welcome ***Sinter Klaas*** on St. Nicholas Eve, December 5th. Dressed as a thinner version of the American Santa Claus, he rides a white schimmel, or horse, accompanied by ***Zwarte Piet***, or Black Peter who is dressed in the clothing of a Spanish Moor. This goes back to the time when the Netherlands were under Spanish rule.

Black Peter does most of the heavy lifting, so to speak, for Sinter Klaas, and carries a bulging sack of gifts for the children. The children leave their shoes and a drawing for Sinter Klaas and carrots and hay for his horse in hopes of receiving a gift.

The people of the Netherlands enjoy a festive meal and exchange gifts, but they do so after staging elaborate pranks, such as hiding the gifts throughout the house; a sort of treasure hunt!

The merriment of this holiday makes St. Nicholas Day the children's favorite of the five national festival days observed by the Dutch.

Eventually, St. Nicholas came to the New World, or the ***United States***. This had a great deal to do with the Dutch settlers who came to this country in the 17th century.

When the Dutch came to the New World, their lead ship had a figure head, or statue, on its bow of St. Nicholas, or as the Dutch called him, Sinter Klaas, the patron saint of sailors. This was to guarantee the ship safe passage. When the Dutch arrived in the New World, they gave thanks to the Patron Saint of Sailors for their safe arrival.

St. Nicholas' influence continued far beyond that of the safe arrival of ships. As retold in Washington Irving's famous book ***Diedriech Knickerbocker: An History of New York City from the Beginning of the World to the End of the Dutch Dynasty*** Oloffe Van Kortland, a member of the Dutch development council, was asked to choose a site for a new city. Van Kortland went in search of an appropriate area and promptly fell asleep in the woods. He awoke when he heard the sound of sleigh bells. He looked up in the sky and saw a miniature sleigh pulled by reindeer above the treetops. Soon it landed in a clearing and out of the sleigh hopped Sinter Klaas.

He came to Van Kortland and said he would assist him in finding the ideal location to establish what would become the greatest city in the New World.

Sinter Klaas gave Van Kortland very specific instructions. Sinter Klass told Van Kortland, "I will take a drag of my pipe, and blow the smoke into the air. You are to follow that smoke until it settles on the ground. Where that smoke settles, I want you to establish the city of New Amsterdam". Van Kortland followed Sinter Klaas' instructions exactly.

When all was said and done, New Amsterdam was established, and became one of the busier cities in the New World. As thanks to Sinter Klaas for help in establishing the city of New Amsterdam, the people of the city made St. Nicholas its patron saint.

Eventually, people of many countries came to New Amsterdam. Many of them were British. They eventually became the leaders of the town and on June 12th, 1665, New Amsterdam was renamed New York in honor of the King of England's brother, the Duke of York.

The British did not however, change their patron saint. St. Nicholas remains to this very day the patron saint of New York City.

To date, there are six churches of various denominations dedicated to St. Nicholas in the city of New York. One of them, *The Collegiate Church of St. Nicholas* (Reformed Church in America) can trace its roots back to the original St. Nicholas Church established by the Dutch in New Amsterdam.

Time passed, and more and more immigrants came from England to New York City. The English did not speak Dutch, so rather than call St. Nicholas Sinter Klaas; they began to call him **Santa Claus**.

In 1822, Clement C. Moore wrote a poem for his children about a Christmas visit from St. Nicholas. In this poem, he talked about a jolly old elf that came down the chimney and filled the children's stockings.

Many of Mr. Moore's friends asked for copies of his poem and in 1823, one of these friends published the poem anonymously in the Troy, New York Sentinel. It later became popularly known by its first line ***"T'was the night Before Christmas"***.

As more immigrants came to America, they brought with them their own traditions of St. Nicholas. Decorating Christmas trees, hanging stockings and giving gifts are all traditions brought from the celebrations of St. Nicholas throughout Europe.

All of these wonderful celebrations are still celebrated to this day. Many children put out their shoes on December 5th for St. Nicholas Day. Many oldest daughters adorned in white gowns and candle lit wreaths bring their parents breakfast on December 13th for St. Lucia Day.

The main holiday for many people is the birth date of Jesus on December 25th Christmas Day. There are others that celebrate the coming of the Magi, or the Epiphany on January 6th.

It doesn't really matter when you celebrate; all of these wonderful feasts celebrate the Christmas Season.

Alabama was the first state to recognize Christmas as an official holiday. This tradition began in 1836.

4. Symbols and Traditions of Christmas

Throughout history, there have been many symbols and traditions related to Christmas that have made their way into our celebrations. The United States is a wonderful melting pot of nationalities and cultures. The people of these cultures brought with them their own traditions of Christmas.

The Christmas Tree

There is nothing more beautiful than a brightly lit Christmas tree twinkling with holiday cheer! Why do we decorate trees? When did this tradition begin?

The Christmas tree is symbol that dates back to the pagan traditions of worshipping the spirits of the forest. In the dead of winter, the one thing that had life was the evergreen. Pagans worshipped the tree that appeared to remain living when all else seemed to be dead. St. Nicholas took some of the pagan's rituals, and brought them into the Christian tradition, while trying to convert the pagans to Christianity. He thought that if the pagans saw some familiar symbols, they would feel more comfortable, and therefore more open to the teachings of Nicholas.

Later, the first person credited with decorating a Christmas tree with lights was the German theologian Martin Luther. The regions of Germany began decorating the trees with candles. Glass blowers took their art and applied it to the celebration by making beautiful blown glass ornaments to make the trees even more beautiful!

In the early part of the 19th century, England's Queen Victoria married a German prince by the name of Albert. Albert brought with him the Christmas traditions of his own country by having the first Christmas tree in England, decorated with the ornaments and candles from his beloved Germany.

The tradition made its way across the Atlantic to the United States. Today, people of the U.S. have made Christmas trees an important part of the celebration; decorating their trees with ornaments, lights, tinsel and garland.

Christmas Wreaths, Holly and Mistletoe

St. Nicholas took other pagan symbols of evergreen, holly and mistletoe and made them symbols of Christmas. Again, Nicholas used these symbols to convert the pagans to Christianity. In England, Father Christmas wears a wreath of evergreen in this hair. Today, Christmas wreaths symbolize the continuing circle of Christ's love.

The tradition of holly at Christmastime actually symbolizes the crown of thorns Jesus was forced to wear on his head at his crucifixion, while its red berries remind one of the blood which Christ had to shed for the world. As in many homes around the world-- in France, people hang holly in their homes as a symbol to others that they celebrate Christ's birth.

Mistletoe was the strongest of the pagan symbols. It was believed to contain a very powerful spirit. The pagans, particularly of Norse and Celtic traditions, considered it good luck to hang mistletoe in their homes.

Nicholas's teaching of the mistletoe brought its meaning to be of peace and goodwill. Today, many stand under the greenery in hopes of receiving a kiss!

Christmas Stockings / Shoes

Both of these symbols date back to the story of Bishop Nicholas saving the three daughters of the man who had fallen on hard times. In some countries, people believe the money in the handkerchief Nicholas threw in the window landed in the shoes of the three daughters. Others believe it landed in stockings drying by the fire. This is the reason why some people put out shoes for St. Nicholas Day, and others hang their stockings by the fireplace on Christmas Eve.

The contents of a Christmas stocking or shoe have very traditional meanings, too! In the toe of the stocking is usually an orange. This is a symbol of the money Nicholas threw in the window of the man to save his three daughters. Chocolate coins serve as another reminder of the money thrown in the window by Bishop Nicholas. Stockings may also contain an apple for good health, a small bit of coal as a reminder that no child is perfectly good, small simple toys, and at the top of the stocking candy, sweets, nuts and other treats. Many of these treats are found by children who are visited by St. Nicholas.

Candy Canes

In regions of Europe, candy makers bent the end of a peppermint stick as a reminder of Nicholas' bishop's staff. The peppermint sticks were given as a treat to performers of traditional mummer's plays. A mummer's play was a very popular form of St. Nicholas Day celebrations.

In these plays, ordinary citizens (mummers) would reenact stories of the life and miracles of St. Nicholas.

Some of the more popular stories involved the saving of three students from the evil butcher, Pere Frouttard who had placed them in the pickle barrel as well as the raising of the dead of the Egyptian sailor, the saving of the three innocents (generals), and the return of a kidnapped child of Myra to his parents on the Feast of St. Nicholas.

Today, the colors of the candy canes are said to be symbolic of the purity and blood of Jesus.

Oranges

An orange in a stocking is a reminder of the story of the three daughters. They represent the bags of money that St. Nicholas threw through the window to save them from slavery. Another legend refers to the fact that many years ago; fruit was not as plentiful as it is today. To receive a piece of fruit was to receive something as precious as gold.

Gold Coins

This symbol also refers to that miraculous story of St. Nicholas saving the three daughters from slavery by throwing the handkerchiefs or bags of gold into the window to save them from being sold.

The Miracle of Three

The number three is very common in the legends and symbols of Nicholas. The miracle of the number three goes back to the Nicene Council of 325AD. This council or meeting of Christian bishops was called by Emperor Constantine. During these meetings, Nicholas wanted the Holy Trinity (Father, Son and Holy Spirit) to be considered equal. Arias, a bishop from Egypt argued that the Son Jesus and the Holy Spirit were not equal to God the Father.

Other stories of Nicholas refer to the number three—the three students in the pickle barrel, the three generals, the three daughters, etc.

This reinforced Nicholas' teaching of the Holy Trinity and its importance to the Christian faith.

If you ever see a picture or statue of Bishop Nicholas, he is often portrayed holding three gold balls. Can you guess what the three gold balls symbolize? They represent the three bags of gold thrown in the window of the man down on his luck with no dowry for his daughters.

St. Nicholas Day Celebrations

Celebrations of St. Nicholas became very popular in his hometown of Myra. These celebrations go back centuries. There is a story of a young boy in Myra who was watching his family's house while his parents were in the town centre for the Feast of St. Nicholas. During the celebration, pirates from the island of Crete snuck into town, and robbed the cathedral and the houses of the people attending the celebrations. When they came to the boy's house, they kidnapped him, brought him to Crete, and made him the official cup bearer to the Emir or King of Crete.

When the parents discovered the boy was missing, his mother blamed it on St. Nicholas and swore never to celebrate the feast day again. After several years, she was convinced by her husband and friends to celebrate in a modest fashion by having a dinner party.

When everyone sat down to eat, a noise came from the courtyard. When the husband went to see what the commotion was about, he saw his long lost son. The child explained that while he was serving the Emir his cup, he felt a tug at his neck. The boy said he was lifted out of the castle, flown through the air and across the sea. He feared for his life, but saw to his right Bishop Nicholas with his arm around him saying "Fear not, I am bringing you home". When his mother heard this, she declared, "St. Nicholas is truly the giver of gifts, and the protector of children. He saved my child from kidnappers, and brought me back the gift of my son, who I thought I had lost forever."

This story is often recreated in the mummer's plays in Europe as part of the St. Nicholas Day celebrations.

After many years, the Christmas season, beginning with St. Nicholas Day began to get a little out of hand. Many people began to make the season more like a Mardi Gras. They completely forgot the religious meaning behind the days leading up to Christmas.

This revelry was most obvious in the celebrations of St. Nicholas Day itself. Parades were held, and a young altar boy would become the "boy bishop". The "boy bishop" had the authority to order the adults around for the day! Eventually, this got completely out of hand and the boy "Nicholas" began to tell the adults to do dangerous things, trying to see what he could get them to do!

Eventually, Church leaders began to limit the celebrations, and brought them back to what they should be-- religious observances and not secular parties.

The bishops reminded the people of the teachings of St. Nicholas, which were to honor God. The mischievous activities and disruptive, roving groups of children causing trouble-- while they were supposedly collecting alms for the poor, a practice that had become popular with the celebrations-- were not appropriate.

Today, some St. Nicholas Day celebrations are as simple as children leaving shoes out for a simple trinket from the saint. The celebration encourages children to do a good deed in Nicholas' name during the long season of Advent—expecting nothing in return!

 Telesphorus, the second Bishop of Rome (125-136 AD) declared that public Church services should be held to celebrate "The Nativity of our Lord and Saviour." In 320 AD, Pope Julius I and other religious leaders specified 25 December as the official date of the birth of Jesus Christ.

5. The Twelve Days of Christmas and the Christmas Season

The blessed season of Christmas begins with the first Sunday of Advent four weeks before Christmas, and continues with the feast day of St. Nicholas on December 6th, St. Lucia Day on December 13th, Christmas on December 25th, and finally concludes with the Epiphany on January 6th.

The word Advent comes from the Latin word *adventus* which means "coming". It is a liturgical season celebrated in many western Christian churches. It is a time of waiting and preparation of the birth of Jesus on Christmas Day.

The twelve days between Christmas Day and the Epiphany are known as the "Twelve Days of Christmas". While each of the twelve days has been touted in song for many years, it was actually written in the 18th century to help Catholic children in England remember articles of faith during the persecution by Protestant monarchs. Any written evidence of Catholic teaching was considered illegal.

The term "true love" was meant to represent God and each of the gifts various ideas. The partridge in a pear tree symbolized Christ.

- ❖ 2 Turtle Doves were the Old and New Testaments
- ❖ 3 French Hens were the Theological Virtues of Faith, Hope and Charity
- ❖ 4 Calling Birds represented the Four Gospels and/or the Four Evangelists
- ❖ 5 Golden Rings were the first Five Books of the Old Testament, the "Pentateuch", which relays the history of man's fall from grace.
- ❖ 6 Geese A-laying symbolized the six days of Creation
- ❖ 7 Swans A-swimming stood for the seven gifts of the Holy Spirit, and the seven sacraments
- ❖ 8 Maids A-milking were the eight beatitudes
- ❖ 9 Ladies Dancing represented the nine Fruits of the Holy Spirit
- ❖ 10 Lords A-leaping signify the ten commandments
- ❖ 11 Pipers Piping suggest the eleven faithful apostles

❖ 12 Drummers Drumming signify the twelve points of doctrine in the Apostle's Creed

There is a belief that the partridge in the Twelve Days of Christmas is meant to symbolize Christ and the pear tree his cross.

Epilogue

St. Nicholas of Myra became a saint because of the miracles he performed. He continues to perform miracles today in the form of the goodwill that seems to permeate the world at Christmas. People who might not get along at any other time of year, or people who might walk by a homeless person without a thought, take the time at Christmas to say a kind word, or to give some money with a message of encouragement. That is truly the miracle of Christmas.

There are many other celebrations of St. Nicholas and Christmas throughout the world. In the Southern Hemisphere, Christmas is a summer holiday!

In South America, the *presepio*, or nativity plays a very important part in the celebrations. The presepio is part of a series of novenas, and public gatherings of worship in the form of prayer, hymns, and religious poetry usually in a nine-day period or morning church services, or re-enactment plays and pageants of the nativity scenes recalling the journey of the Holy Family to Bethlehem under the guidance of angels and the Christmas star.

In South Africa, the most important part of their Christmas worship service is the *love offering*, this is the gift in honor of Jesus. At about 8 or 9 o'clock everyone makes their way to the celebration of the birthday of Jesus. Everyone who attends the service goes forward to lay down their gift upon the raised platform near the Communion table. Not one person will attend the service without giving a gift.

No matter where in the world St. Nicholas travels, it is important to remember through all of the gift giving, music, and food that make the holiday season so festive, that he wants us *all* to look out for the other person, show some kindness, and as he told the man whose daughters received the bags of gold for their dowries—if you want to make me happy, do good deeds for others expecting *nothing* in return, and you will be rewarded tenfold. Merry Christmas!

Family Recipes

Traditional food is a very important part of any holiday, especially Christmas! The aroma of our favorite holiday foods can bring to mind wonderful memories of past Christmases. Here are a few of our favorite holiday recipes passed down through the generations in our families. Add your own on the following pages.

The origin of the cookies lies in the Medieval European recipes. Lebkuchen (gingerbread) was probably the first cake/cookie to be traditionally related with Christmas. Cookies spread all over Europe by 1500. Therefore every house made or baked cookies in great amounts, which were either Lebkuchen or buttery Spritz Cookies.

Grandma's Fruitcake
(In our family for 70 years)

Ingredients

- 12oz jar of unsweetened applesauce
- 2 cups sugar
- 1 cup butter or margarine
- 3 cups sifted flour
- 1 Tbsp. baking soda
- 1 Tbsp. cinnamon
- 1 Tbsp. vanilla
- 1 pinch salt
- 8oz. Raisins
- 1 oz. container red cherries*
- 1 oz. container green cherries*
- 1 oz. container candied pineapple*

*I usually take ¼ of the 4 oz. round containers of cherries and pineapple that are popular at the holiday.

Procedure

- Preheat oven to 350F.
- All fruit must be cut up very small!
- Combine applesauce, sugar, and butter in a medium saucepan on a very low flame—don't cook it, just melt it.
- Sift all dry ingredients
- Pour heated mixture into a very large bowl.
- SLOWLY add dry ingredients.
- Pour mixture into a lightly greased tube pan.
- Bake for 1 hour and 15 minutes at 350F.
- Check with a toothpick. If the toothpick does not come out clean, return to oven for 10 more minutes.

Grandma's Fudge (In our family for 70 years)

Ingredients

- 2 Cups sugar
- 2 Tbsp. butter
- 2 Squares of **Baker's Bitter Chocolate**
- ¾ Cup Whole Milk
- 1 tsp. vanilla
- Candy thermometer

Procedure

- Over a low flame, combine sugar, chocolate squares, and milk in a medium saucepan.
- Stirring constantly, continue to cook over a low flame until the candy thermometer reads 237F.
- Remove from heat and let cool for 5 minutes, no more.
- After 5 minutes, stir in the butter and vanilla until very thick, but not solid.
- Pour mixture into a greased 13x9 in. pan. Let harden, cut into squares.

This is not your typical soft fudge; it is a bit harder than most. This is why it is so popular in our family!

Before 1886, the origin and history of fudge is unclear, but Fudge is thought to be an American invention. Most believe the first batch was a result of a accidental "fudged" batch of caramels, hence the name "fudge".

Grandma's Date Nut Logs
(In our family for 60 years)

Ingredients

- 1 cup dates (cut up)
- ¼ cup butter
- 1 tsp vanilla
- 1 egg
- 1 cup chopped walnuts
- 2 cups Rice Krispies cereal
- Shredded coconut

Procedure

- Combine all ingredients
- Cook mixture in a medium saucepan on a low flame until thick.
- Shape into 1-2in. logs
- Roll logs in shredded coconut
- Cool logs on a greased cookie sheet
- Store logs in an air tight contain

Christmas 20__

Location & Who was there

_____
_____
_____
_____
_____
_____
_____
_____

The Weather that day was

_____
_____
_____

Wonderful Memories

Christmas 20__

Location & Who was there

_____
_____
_____
_____
_____
_____
_____

The Weather that day was

_____
_____
_____

Wonderful Memories

Christmas 20__

Location & Who was there

_____
_____
_____
_____
_____
_____
_____

The Weather that day was

_____
_____
_____

Wonderful Memories

Christmas 20__

Location & Who was there

_____
_____
_____
_____
_____
_____
_____

The Weather that day was

_____
_____
_____

Wonderful Memories

Christmas 20__

Location & Who was there
_____
_____
_____
_____
_____
_____
_____

The Weather that day was
_____
_____
_____

Wonderful Memories

Family Recipes

Family Recipes

Family Recipes

Family Recipes

Family Recipes

Recommended Reading

Merck, Tim, Beth Merck, and Elizabeth Johnson. *Origins and Legends of Father Christmas: a Collection of Much-loved Traditions and Stories.* Spokane, WA: Merck Family's Old World Christmas, 2000. Print.

The Santa Map. Minneapolis: Hedberg Maps. Print.

Naythons, Matthew. *Christmas around the World.* San Francisco, CA: Collins San Francisco, 1996. Print.

McKnight, George Harley. *St. Nicholas: His Legend and His Role in the Christmas Celebration and Other Popular Customs.* Gansevoort, NY: Corner House Historical Publications, 1996. Print.

Mayer, Marianna. *The Real Santa Claus.* New York: Phyllis Fogelman, 2001. Print.

Bowler, G. Q. *The World Encyclopedia of Christmas.* Toronto: M&S, 2004. Print.

Yzermans, Vincent Arthur. *Wonderworker: the True Story of How Saint Nicholas Became Santa Claus.* Chicago, IL: ACTA Publications, 2004. Print.

"Christmas Traditions Around the World." *PortHarbor -the Main Entrance to a Unique Cybercommunity.* Web. 04 Nov. 2010.

<http://www.portharbor.com/santa/xsatrad.php#Spain>.

"Santa Claus Facts, Origins, Christmas Celebration in Different Countries, and Fun Tidbits." *Austin Web Design - Austin Website Hosting - Lone Star Internet.* Web. 04 Nov. 2010. <http://www.lone-star.net/mall/main-areas/santafaq.htm>.

"Christmas Around The World." *TheHolidaySpot: Holidays and Festivals Celebrations, Greeting Cards, Activities, Crafts, Recipes Wallpapers, and More.* Web. 04 Nov. 2010. <http://www.theholidayspot.com/christmas/worldxmas/>.

http://www.newseum.org/yesvirginia/

http://www.stnicholascenter.org/Brix?pageID=23

Book Terry Lynch to Speak to Your Organization

Speaker Terry Lynch developed his program: *"The Legend of St Nicholas"* to bring the history and traditions of the holiday season to all ages. Through historical portrayal, Terry brings St. Nicholas, the giver of gifts and protector of children on his journey throughout the world and brings his message of love and acceptance to young and old. History happens when you least expect it!

For many years, Terry an actor, and his wife Laura, a certified educator, have combined their careers to write books and develop programs that not only educate, but entertain. For availability and booking information, you can contact Terry & Laura Lynch through their websites www.hfkpresents.com or www.historiesforkids.com email at info@hfkpresents.com, or directly at: 708-218-7001.

Check out **HFK Presents: 5 Minutes of History** on the HFK YouTube Channel at: http://www.youtube.com/user/HFKPresents.